D1389122

HIRE
AND
KEEP
THE
BEST PEOPLE

BOOKS BY BRIAN TRACY

Advanced Selling Strategies

Eat That Frog!

Effective Leadership

Focal Point

Get Paid More and Promoted Faster

The Gift of Self-Confidence

The Great Big Book of Wisdom

Little Silver Book of Prosperity

Mastering Your Time

Maximum Achievement

*The 100 Absolutely Unbreakable Laws
of Business Success*

The Peak Performance Woman

The 21 Success Secrets of Self-Made Millionaires

Personal Achievement

Success Is a Journey

Successful Selling

A Treasury of Personal Achievement

Universal Laws of Success

COAUTHORED BY BRIAN TRACY

Speaking Secrets of the Masters

Insights into Excellence

HIRE
AND
KEEP
THE
BEST PEOPLE

21 PRACTICAL AND PROVEN TECHNIQUES YOU CAN USE IMMEDIATELY

BRIAN TRACY

BK

BERRETT-KOEHLER PUBLISHERS, INC.
San Francisco

Berrett-Koehler Publishers, Inc.
235 Montgomery Street, Suite 650
San Francisco, CA 94104-2916
Tel: (415) 288-0260   Fax: (415) 362-2512   www.bkconnection.com

ORDERING INFORMATION

Quantity sales. Special discounts are available on quantity purchases by corporations, associations, and others. For details, contact the "Special Sales Department" at the Berrett-Koehler address above.

Individual sales. Berrett-Koehler publications are available through most bookstores. They can also be ordered direct from Berrett-Koehler: Tel: (800) 929-2929; Fax: (802) 864-7626; www.bkconnection.com

Orders for college textbook/course adoption use. Please contact Berrett-Koehler: Tel: (800) 929-2929; Fax: (802) 864-7626.

Orders by U.S. trade bookstores and wholesalers. Please contact Publishers Group West, 1700 Fourth Street, Berkeley, CA 94710. Tel: (510) 528-1444; Fax: (510) 528-3444.

Printed in the United States of America

Printed on acid-free and recycled paper that is composed of 50% recovered fiber, including 10% postconsumer waste.

Library of Congress Cataloging-in-Publication Data
Tracy, Brian.
   Hire and keep the best people : 21 practical and proven techniques you
use immediately / by Brian Tracy.
      p. cm.
   Includes bibliographical references and index.
   ISBN 1-57675-169-4
   1. Employee selection. 2. Employees—Recruiting. 3. Employee retention.
   4. Personnel management. I. Title.

HF5549.S.S38 T7 2001
658.3'11-dc21   2001043378

Copyediting and proofreading by PeopleSpeak.
Book design and composition by Beverly Butterfield, Girl of the West Productions.

FIRST EDITION
06 05 04 03 02 01   10 9 8 7 6 5 4 3 2 1

This book is fondly dedicated to my good friend, partner, business associate, and all-around excellent executive, Cam Framer, from whom I've learned so much about the art and science of management.

Contents

Preface

This book is for every manager, supervisor, entrepreneur, or executive who has ever had to hire people as part of his or her job. In each chapter, you will learn key ideas, methods, and techniques that you can use immediately to hire better people and improve their job performance once they begin and ever afterward.

Most people become managers accidentally. As the result of success, experience, promotion, or necessity, they find themselves responsible for the work of others. They have to find, interview, hire, and assign people whose work performance determines their own success. Their pay and promotion depend on the way that the people they have chosen do their jobs.

None of us is properly prepared in advance to select and keep the best people. It is both an art and a skill that can be learned only in the crucible of experience—and as the result of numerous mistakes. Often we look upon a vacancy as a problem to be solved as quickly as possible so we can get back to our "real" jobs. We overlook the fact that selecting the right people is at the core of our real jobs.

Once they have hired someone, rightly or wrongly, many managers are unclear or unaware of exactly what they can do and say to the employee to build and maintain loyalty, commitment, and enthusiasm for the job and the company. As a result, they often do and say things that hurt productivity and performance instead of increasing it.

If you recognize yourself in this description, this book is for you. It gives you a series of time-tested, proven strategies that work quickly to improve your performance in hiring good people in the first place and then getting the best out of them once they have started work.

You won't find any great breakthroughs or secret formulas in the pages ahead. There are no abstract theories or complex systems. What you will learn are practical principles that are simple and fast acting. They will equip you to get better results from the first minute you apply them.

Most managers, no matter how experienced they are, do not know or do not practice these principles. They hire in a random fashion, relying on intuition and superficial clues from the candidates. They are uncomfortable with the process and try to get it over with as quickly as possible.

Once they have hired someone, they manage and motivate the employee in a random and haphazard way. Many managers actually look upon these interpersonal activities as distractions from their busy schedules, to be completed quickly so they can get back to work.

As you read this book, your attitude toward hiring and retention will change in a positive way. You will learn how to become an excellent manager in these key performance areas that determine your success in your career more than anything else you do. In one hour of reading, you will come up to speed on the critical ideas of *hiring* and *keeping* people practiced by the best managers in the best companies everywhere.

By faithfully referring to this book and by practicing the principles you learn, you will become one of the most effective managers in your industry. Your contribution to your organization will increase in value. Your sense of satisfaction and feeling of competence will grow. Your ability to get things done through others, faster and easier, will expand beyond your current level of performance and ability. Your future as a manager, supervisor, entrepreneur, or executive will become unlimited.

Brian Tracy
Solana Beach, California
July 2001

Introduction:
The Critical Skill

The critical constraint on the growth and success of your business, or any business, is the ability to attract and keep good people. All other resources are freely available and can be acquired with relative ease. You can get all the capital, real estate, furniture, fixtures, manufacturing and distribution equipment, and packaging and marketing materials you need. But what makes all these factors productive and profitable is the quality of the people behind them, and there has never been such a shortage of high-quality people as we are experiencing today.

Employers in the twenty-first century have to make a major mental paradigm shift. They have to direct their thinking completely away from earlier times, when plenty of capable people were available, to the current situation, where the number of good people is quite limited. In making this shift, employers have to direct their attention toward hiring and keeping good people and focus on that goal as a major responsibility of management. This may be the most important responsibility of all.

In the course of my thirty-year career, I have personally started, built, managed, or turned around twenty-two different businesses. I have consulted for more than five hundred corporations and trained thousands of managers and executives in the key skills of finding and keeping good people.

I have found that attracting good people and getting them to stay is a key business skill, perhaps *the* key business skill. The good news is that, like all business skills, it is *learnable* by virtually anyone through practice and repetition. Countless managers have developed this skill to such a high level that they consistently make good hires, year after year.

Meanwhile, other managers have not yet mastered this critical skill. As a result, they fumble through interviews, hire largely on the basis of guesswork and intuition, and are constantly amazed when as many as 70 percent of their hires don't work out. They often compound this inadequacy by blaming their poor hiring decisions on the people they have hired, thereby making it almost impossible for them to learn and grow from their mistakes.

However, the truth is that if an incompetent or inappropriate person is hired, it is the *manager* who is incompetent, not the employee. The fact is that hiring is a key managerial skill. If someone consistently hires people who cannot or will not do the job properly, the manager should be replaced before he or she does irreparable damage to the company. Many businesses flounder and go under because of the incompetence of a single key person in a key job, placed and kept there by an incompetent superior.

In the pages ahead, I will share with you twenty-one of the greatest ideas ever discovered to help you to become vastly better at hiring and keeping the people you need to make your business a success. By practicing these principles, you will become one of the best managers of your generation. You will make an extraordinary contribution to your organization and become invaluable to your company.

Make Selection Your Top Priority

The selection process is the key to your success and to the success of your company. Nothing is more important to your future than your ability to select the right people to work with you to make that future a reality. A mistake in selection, in itself, can lead to underachievement and failure in a critical area and often to the failure of the entire organization.

The first Law of Management concerns selection. Fully 95 percent of the success of any enterprise is determined by the people chosen to work in that enterprise in the first place. If you get this right, everything else will usually work out all right as well. If you select the wrong people, nothing else will work.

The rule is that if you select in *haste,* you will repent at *leisure.* Many of your worst problems in business will come from having hired a person too quickly. Once the person has started the job and turns out to be inappropriate, you then have to spend considerable time, energy, and emotion justifying your decision and dealing with the difficulties of having the wrong person in place.

One of the rules for good hiring is this: "Hire slowly and fire fast." Take your time to make the right decision prior to hiring in the first place. But if it becomes clear that you have made a mistake, move quickly to reassign or get rid of the person before he or she does any more harm.

I have hired someone on a Monday and fired him on Tuesday, as soon as it became clear that I had made a mistake. Remember, people always look the very best during the first job interview. They will say or promise almost anything to get hired in the first place, but as soon as you give them an actual job to do, they often turn out to be very different from what you expected or from what they led you to expect.

The very best time to fire a person is the first time the thought crosses your mind. If you have made a poor selection decision, don't compound the mistake by keeping the wrong person in that job. Have the courage and common sense to admit that you have made a mistake, correct the mistake, and get on with the business of running an efficient, effective workforce.

Hiring is an art. It cannot be rushed. It requires focus, concentration, and unbroken thought. You must take your time if you really want to hire well.

All personnel decisions require a good deal of reflection before you make them. *Fast* hiring decisions usually turn out to be *wrong* hiring decisions.

A successful manager, a man with a great reputation for having hired many of the top people in his company, told me that he had a simple rule for hiring anyone: Once he had decided upon the candidate, he waited thirty days before he made an offer. He found that the very act of delaying a hiring decision made it a vastly better decision when he finally made it.

This might be a totally inappropriate strategy for you, or for a job candidate, in a dynamic marketplace. Nonetheless, the basic principle of going slow whenever you can is solid and irrefutable. It will greatly increase your overall success rate in hiring.

As a manager, your natural tendency is to hire a person as a solution to a problem, to fill a hole in the lineup, or to do a job that suddenly needs to be done. This is like grabbing a bucket of water and throwing it on a fire. Sometimes, however, if you are not careful, the bucket can turn out to be full of gasoline, and the situation you create can be worse than the situation you are trying to correct.

Ask yourself, honestly, have you ever hired a person quickly with little thought? How often have you had problems as a result? There is nothing wrong with making a mistake as long as you learn from the mistake and do not repeat it. It is true that occasionally you will make a good quick hiring decision, and it will work out well. But this is like a miracle, and as Peter Drucker once wrote, "It is not that miracles don't happen; it is just that you cannot depend upon them."

Poor selection is very expensive. Experts in the field of personnel placement estimate that a wrong hire costs a company three to six times a person's annual compensation. This means that if you hire a person for $50,000 a year and the person does not work out, the overall cost to you and your company can be between $150,000 and $300,000.

What are these costs? First of all, there is your *lost time,* the time that you spend interviewing, hiring, and training the person to get him or her up to speed. There is also the lost time of all the other people who are involved in the hiring process, both inside and outside your organization. When you calculate the hourly rates of these people and add the costs of the work not getting done while the wrong person is being selected, trained, placed, managed, supervised, and eventually fired—with all the attendant costs of separating him or her from the company—the direct and indirect costs can be heartbreaking.

Second, there is your *lost money,* the actual cost of the salary, benefits, and training expenses of the person who eventually doesn't work out. You may even have considerable costs for advertising or placement fees to an outside agency. All this money is wasted in that your company receives no return on investment in terms of actual work performed and results generated. The money is gone forever.

Finally, there is your *lost productivity* while you are busy finding a replacement for the person whom you shouldn't have hired in the first place. In addition, your own personal time, emotion, and energy have been wasted on an activity that actually has had a detrimental effect on your company.

There is also the lost time and productivity of the various people in your organization who get together and talk about the mis-hire. They rehash what happened and feed the rumor mill. Often, they become demoralized when they see people being hired and fired around them and wonder if they might be next. Their productivity suffers as a result.

Companies with high levels of turnover always *underperform* their better-managed competitors. In fact, high levels of staff turnover as the result of poor hiring or poor management of human resources can be fatal to a company. The excessive costs and accompanying confusion and inefficiencies can drive the company into bankruptcy.

The very best companies and the best managers have the best selection processes. This not only saves them a good deal of time and money in personnel costs, but it creates a reputation for them in the marketplace as being good places to work, making it easier for them to attract more and better candidates in the first place.

It therefore behooves you to think carefully before you bring a new person on board. Sometimes the best hiring decision you ever make is the one you decide not to make in the first place.

ACTION EXERCISES

Make a list of three people you have hired in the past who didn't work out, and then write down three lessons you learned from these hiring mistakes. As historian George Santayana wrote, "Those who cannot remember the past are condemned to repeat it." The more time you take to reflect on your mistakes, the more you will learn from every experience.

Make a list of the names of some of the best hires you have ever made. What did these hiring decisions have in common? How could you apply these general principles to a hiring decision you are dealing with today?

Think Through
the Job

Your mind is incredibly powerful—and never more so than when you focus your mental energies, like a laser beam, on a question or problem for a sustained period of time.

Before you begin your search for new employees, take sufficient time to think through the job carefully. Use the 10/90 Rule. This rule says that the first 10 percent of time that you spend thinking and planning will save you 90 percent of the time and effort required to make the right decision and get the right result in the long run. The 10/90 Rule is an incredible time-saver that requires only patience and discipline to make it work for you.

Think through the exact output responsibilities of the job. Begin by imagining that the job is a *pipeline*. What results must come out of the other end of the pipeline for you to know that the person has done the job in an excellent fashion? How will you both be able to determine that the job has been done well? Think in terms of *accomplishments* rather than activities. Think in terms of outputs rather than inputs. Think in terms of measurable results that are clear and objective.

Consider the salary you pay as if you were buying a specific quality and quantity of results in the marketplace. Exactly how will you measure and define these results? How will you know that you have received your money's worth? What standards and benchmarks will you use to determine that the employee has performed well?

Any job description has three parts. First, there are the *results* expected of that position. You must be absolutely clear about these. Second, there are the *skills* necessary to achieve those results. What are they? Third, and perhaps most important, there are the *personality characteristics* of the ideal person for the job and how well he or she will fit in with the rest of the team.

You should begin the process of defining the job by thinking through what the person is expected to accomplish, day in and day out. *Think* on paper. Describe a typical workday and workweek, from morning to night. The clearer you are about the results you require, the easier it will be for you to find the best candidate for the job.

Once you have determined the results required, identify the exact skills that the ideal candidate will have to have in order to get those results. Hire people for what they have *already* done successfully rather than for what they think they can do if given a chance on your payroll. It is true that some companies believe in hiring for personality and attitude and then teaching specific skills. This is a good idea, but nonetheless you should demand a certain *demonstrated* skill level before you select a candidate if you want to hire the best people.

Finally, you should identify the personal attributes or qualities that the ideal candidate will have. Especially, you will want someone who is honest, positive, hardworking, energetic, focused, and open minded. Write these qualities down and organize them in terms of their importance to you and to the job.

Be sure that a *single* person can do the job you are hiring for. Be sure that you are not creating an impossible job and looking for a miracle worker. Sometimes, with rapid change, a job can grow so complex that you need two different people with two different sets of skills and attributes to do it properly. Always consider this a possibility.

The mark of a superior executive is *thoughtfulness.* The very best managers and executives are far more thoughtful when it comes to personnel decisions than are average managers. The more time you spend thinking and reflecting on the person and the job before you hire, the better decision you will make.

◆

ACTION EXERCISES

Think of a particular job opening that you have currently, or a job that is not being done satisfactorily, and define it in terms of the results you would like to see produced in that position.

Make a list of the skills that the ideal candidate would need to have to do that job in an excellent fashion.

Finally, define the job in terms of the personality characteristics the ideal candidate would have. Be sure that the person is the right "fit" for you and your company.

3

Write Out the Job Description

It is surprising how many people advertise for or seek new job candidates without ever taking a few minutes to sit down and write out a clear description of the person they really want.

Something amazing happens between your head and your hand when you write a list of all the qualities that the ideal job candidate would have. You will be astonished at the incredible clarity that develops on the page in front of you. You will find yourself writing key descriptions and details that had not previously occurred to you. Later, you will find that these essential requirements were vital in making the right hiring decision.

Practice *idealization* for the purpose of this exercise. Imagine that you could write a description of the perfect person and hand it over to a special service, and the service would deliver that person to you, exactly to your specifications. Imagine that you were sending in an order for a person and that the exact person you requested would be delivered to your door. What would he or she be like?

What I do prior to starting a search for a new person is to make a list of everything I can possibly think of that the *perfect* person would be, have, and be able to do if I could find him or her. I then circulate this list to the other people in my company who will be working with whoever is chosen. We then review and massage this list. We discuss the characteristics and organize them by priority. In a few minutes, by working collaboratively, we create a comprehensive description of the ideal person we would like to find. We can then write out a detailed description of the job.

Write the job description by making a list of every task the individual will be doing from the time he or she starts in the morning until the time he or she finishes in the evening. What will the candidate be expected to do? Think of the job as a production process and identify each step in the process as a task that must be completed to a particular standard of performance. Identify the key result areas of the job and write them down.

List every function and responsibility that the individual will have to fulfill to do the job properly, from coming in in the morning, checking messages, and responding to telephone calls and e-mails, all the way through to measuring and reporting on his or her progress to his or her superior. Don't leave anything out. A single omission can lead to hiring the wrong person.

We once hired an account executive who had a tremendous track record in sales and account development with another company. She was a star in her industry. We felt lucky to hire her. And yet, within two weeks of starting the job, she fell apart. She became increasingly distraught and angry and eventually quit. What went wrong?

Upon investigation, we found that her previous company had advertised heavily and generated a continuous supply of sales leads, which she simply followed up on. In the job with our company, however, she was responsible for generating her own leads, something she simply could not do because of her inordinate fear of rejection. We had not made that requirement clear enough because we just assumed (big mistake!) that she knew that prospecting was part of the job. As Alexander MacKenzie wrote, "Errant assumptions lie at the root of most failures."

Once you have a description of the ideal candidate and a clear description of everything that the candidate will be expected to do, set priorities on both lists. Decide what is more important and what is less important to success in the position. Use a simple scoring method of one (low priority) to ten (high priority) for each item.

Divide the lists into "musts" and "wants." Some personal qualities and output responsibilities will be absolutely *essential* to the successful performance of the job. Some are quite desirable but they are not absolutely essential. For example, in my ideal candidate descriptions, I always write down that the person lives fairly close to our offices. But this is a preference, not an essential requirement. This is a "want," not a "must." Some of my best people live an hour or more away from the office.

On the other hand, the skill or proven ability to achieve the most important result of the job goes to the top of the list. This is essential. This is a definite "must." Without this ability, the candidate will fail, no matter how many other positive qualities he or she might have.

The clearer you are about your priorities for the job and the ideal person you are seeking, in advance, the more competently you can interview and the better hiring decision you will make.

Think about the people with whom the person will be working. This is as important as any other factor. Everyone has to fit into a team of some kind, and it is absolutely essential that whomever you hire gets along well with his or her coworkers and is accepted by them. A mistake in this area alone can be fatal to the selection process.

Determine what kind of attitude or personality you want the person to have. In my experience, a positive, optimistic, and open-minded attitude is best. As a rule, you should refuse to hire negative or unhappy people, no matter how good they might be technically. They almost always become the cause and source of most of your problems in the workplace.

Finally, consider all of this information and write out a clear, detailed description of the ideal candidate for the position. Write it out exactly as if you were going to be placing this description as an ad in a major publication and it was going to cost you several thousand dollars for a *single* insertion. Begin this description with your requirements in descending order of importance. Put your most important points in the first sentence.

With this written description, you are now ready to cast your net and begin finding the right person for the job.

◆

ACTION EXERCISES

On a sheet of paper, make a list of every single talent, skill, quality, and characteristic you would like to have in the perfect person for a job opening that currently exists in your department. Imagine that you have no limitations on the quality of candidates available.

Review your list and divide 100 points among the various requirements you have listed. For example, current successful experience in doing exactly the job you need done could be worth 50 points. Living near your office could be worth 1 point.

Select the five to ten most important qualities and build your job description around these elements. Review them with your coworkers. Be sure that everyone is clear about and in agreement with the person you are looking for.

4

Cast a Wide Net

Recruiting and hiring is an ongoing responsibility of management, like answering the telephone and replying to requests. Just as a company is seeking new customers all day, every day, managers must be looking for new people constantly. A lack of talented people is the only real constraint on your ability to get more and better results.

Once upon a time, in those distant days that are gone forever, we would start looking for a person only when we had an opening or a need for that person. Today, however, you must be in a "permanent hiring mode." You must scan your world like radar scans the horizon, continually looking for more and better people to work for you. It is a never-ending job, the success of which will largely determine your success as an executive or an entrepreneur.

An important part of the selection process is generating a sufficient number of suitable candidates from which to choose. The greater the number of good candidates you can find, the more likely it is that you will hire and keep the very best people.

Fortunately, you can find good people in many places. The first place to look is *within* your own company, within your own staff or personnel department. Conduct an *internal* search for the kind of person you are looking for before you consider going outside. Circulate the written job description you have developed throughout your company and tell everyone that you are looking for someone who fits this description.

The general rule is that the average person knows about 300 other people by their first names. When everyone on your staff knows that you are looking for a particular type of person for a job, all will be alert to and aware of coming across that kind of person in the course of their activities.

Many companies today offer hiring bonuses to their staff if they can find a job candidate who will fill a particular position. If you offer your people a bonus for finding someone whom you can hire, you will have every staff member out looking and directing people toward you.

One company fills more than 90 percent of its continuous requirements for additional people by using this method. It pays a $500 bonus for every person hired who was referred by a staff member. It pays an additional $500 if the person is still on the job after six months, and it pays another $500 if the person works for the company for a year. This method has assured the company a steady stream of good candidates and saves it a fortune in advertising and placement fees.

Another great source of job candidates is your personal contacts. Most new hires come through references and referrals from others. Once you have a written job description, get in touch with all the people you know who might run across the kind of candidate you are seeking. Tell them what kind of person you are looking for and ask them to send anyone to you who they feel might fit that description.

Tell your customers, your bankers, your suppliers, your friends, your acquaintances, and even people whom you deal with on an occasional basis, such as your lawyers, accountants, business associates, and so on. Cast your net as widely as possible.

Another excellent source of high-quality people is executive recruiters and placement agencies. Depending on the size of your business, executive recruiters and placement agencies can save you an enormous amount of time, money, and effort in sorting through and finding the kind of people you need to help you grow your business. The key to using these agencies is for you to have a very clear written description of the kind of person you want. Make it easy for them to conduct their searches and to identify the people within their databases who would be suitable for the job you are offering.

Newspaper ads are another source of candidates. The Sunday employment section is the best place to run an ad. The key is to be specific in the job description in your ad and then to prescreen the people who respond to the ad based on the requirements that you have written down. Fully 85 percent of people who respond to newspaper ads are not suitable and can be screened out when they call or send you their resume. If you provide a checklist, your secretary or executive assistant can perform this screening function for you.

Perhaps the most important and fastest growing source of job candidates is the Internet. One-eighth of new jobs are already being filled from Internet advertising today, up from zero just a few years ago. The Internet sites devoted to helping companies find good people are fast, efficient, and inexpensive and reach all over the country. They should be a vital part of your hiring activities. Your company's Internet site should have a button, "Positions Open," that opens a Web page with descriptions of the jobs available and an application form the candidate can complete and submit.

Whether or not you use the Internet, many employers today are requesting that inquiries and job applications be submitted via the Internet rather than by mail. This process demonstrates the level of computer and Internet proficiency of the candidate. It also enables busy managers to review several applications quickly and respond rapidly.

Often overlooked sources of good job candidates are local community colleges. The average age of people attending community college is about twenty-eight years old. The primary reason they are attending is to upgrade their skills so they can get better jobs paying more money. They are self-disciplined self-starters, as demonstrated by the fact that they are taking courses in the first place. They are showing a high degree of personal initiative, which is just what you are looking for.

Contact one or more local community colleges and ask to speak to the placement officer. Tell this person that you are seeking a specific candidate for a specific position. Send the placement officer a copy of your written job description with a covering letter. You might even want to visit him or her personally. Ask the placement officer to refer suitable candidates to you for interviews. This strategy can be very effective.

Finding appropriate candidates is time consuming. It often requires several months to find a key person for an important job. Recruiting should not be left till the last minute. It is an activity that you should get started on immediately, preferably well in advance of when a particular person or skill will be required.

◆

ACTION EXERCISES

Take copies of the written job description to your next staff meeting and circulate them to all attendees. Invite their questions and comments. Ask them to keep an eye open for a candidate who fits the description. You may by surprised at what they suggest or whom they come across in their daily activities.

Visit your local community college and meet the placement officer. Tell the placement officer about your company and ask him or her to recommend anyone to you who fits the description of the person you are looking for.

Create a bonus system in your company for employees who find new candidates for the job openings you have. Get everyone on your staff working to help you find and keep more of the best people.

5

Interview Effectively

Most executives have never been taught how to properly interview people for a position. Fortunately, the most effective interviewing process is quite simple, as long as you can discipline yourself to learn it and then to follow it each time.

Start the process by writing out a logical sequence for the interview. You can even make a brief checklist that you review before you speak to a job candidate for the first time. The first questions are aimed at getting information about the *work experience* of the candidate as it applies to the job under consideration. Then ask questions to ascertain the *skill level* of the candidate. You want to know what his or her *career aspirations* are with regard to this job and your company. Finally, you want to know about his or her work *habits* and attitudes toward this job and toward his or her future.

A variety of excellent assessment instruments and personality tests are available that you can use to get a better feeling for the suitability of the candidate. In my business, we use various instruments with each person, score them, and give copies of the results to the candidate. We then discuss the findings with the candidate in a spirit of open inquiry, mutually seeking the best way to interpret them as they relate to the job under consideration.

Start the interview by putting the candidate at ease and helping him or her to relax. Tell the candidate that this is just an "exploratory interview" and that your mutual goal is to see if what you are offering and what the candidate is looking for are the same thing.

Here is another rule: "Don't start selling until you have decided to buy." In other words, resist the temptation to begin the interview by telling the candidate what a great job is being offered and what a great company you have *before* you have concluded that this is the kind of person you want to hire in the first place.

The key to good interviewing is for you to ask good questions and then listen carefully and patiently to the answers. Pause before replying. Allow silences in the conversation. Question for clarification. Ask, "What do you mean?" regularly.

Never assume that you know or understand what is said until you have checked to be sure. Use open-ended questions that begin with the words *who, how, why, when, where,* and *what* to elicit as much information as possible. For example, you can ask:

1. What were your primary responsibilities at your last job? At the job before that?
2. Whom did you report to and how was your relationship with your boss?
3. Why did you take that job and how do you feel it worked out for you?
4. What did you enjoy the most about your last job? What did you do best?
5. What are the most important lessons you've learned in your career so far?

Remember that the person who asks questions has control of the interview. Be sure that it is you.

The more a person talks, the better feeling you will get about whether or not he or she is a good candidate for the job. And you learn only when you are listening. You don't learn anything when you are talking about yourself, the company, or the job.

There is a simple formula you can use in an interview. It is called the "Swan Formula" and comes from executive recruiter John Swan. It is based on the letters *S-W-A-N*. These stand for the four ingredients you are looking for: Smart, Work Hard, Ambitious, and Nice.

How *smart* the candidate is, his or her level of intelligence, is very important in determining how well he or she will do the job. According to the work by Daniel Seligman, writer for *Fortune* magazine for many years and now with *Forbes* magazine, IQ alone will account for fully 72 percent of a person's ability to do the job. Perhaps the simplest way for you to assess intelligence is to listen to the number and type of questions that he or she asks. Intelligent people are usually curious and continually ask you about yourself and the company.

You also want people who are willing to *work hard,* above and beyond normal working hours, whenever it is required. You don't want a person who is intelligent, ambitious, nice, and *lazy.* A good question to ask is, "How would you feel about working evenings or weekends if there was an important job that had to be done on a tight schedule?" A candidate's answer can be quite revealing, whether or not you will ever need the person to work overtime.

An *ambitious* candidate is a person who wants to move ahead rapidly in his or her career and who sees this job as an opportunity or a springboard to something even better if he or she does it well. One measure of ambition is whether the person asks a lot of questions about the future, both of the company and the job, and what he or she has to do to earn more money or get promoted. A good question to ask to check for ambition is, "Where would you ideally like to be in your career in three to five years?"

Finally, always look for and hire *nice* people. A pleasant personality is perhaps as important as any other quality you can find in a good job candidate. An optimistic person is generally warm and friendly throughout the interview and is comfortable with himself or herself with you. Look for this attitude in every interview.

Here are some other qualities to look for in the interview. First of all, look for achievement or *result orientation*. When you ask questions, listen for examples from the person's background where he or she has really enjoyed succeeding and getting results at a previous job. The only real predictor of future performance is past performance. Probe this area carefully and demand specifics, not generalities: "What exactly did you do and what results did you get?"

Second, listen for intelligent questions. As mentioned above, one of the hallmarks of intelligence is *curiosity*. One of the hallmarks of curiosity is that a good candidate will have a series of questions, usually written out, that he or she wants to ask about you, the company, the job, opportunities for the future, and so on. Ask, "What questions do you have about the company or the job?"

Third, look for a *sense of urgency*. A good question you can ask to test for a sense of urgency is, "If we were to offer you this job, how soon would you be prepared to start?" Even if you are not ready to make a hiring decision, this question often reveals a lot about the candidate.

The right candidate will want to start as soon as possible. The wrong candidate will have all kinds of reasons for delaying a decision or delaying leaving a current employer. The worst candidates of all are usually those who want to take a vacation before they begin working for you.

Remember, *fast* personnel decisions are almost invariably *wrong* personnel decisions. Proceed slowly. Be patient. Ask good questions and listen carefully to the answers. Take notes when the person talks. Ask questions to get more information about the highest priority items in your job description. Ask how the candidate feels he or she would perform in those areas.

Only when you have reached the conclusion that this is the kind of person you would like to hire should you tell him or her more details about the company and the job. Start selling only when you have decided to buy.

◆

ACTION EXERCISES

Plan your next interview in advance. Make a list of questions that you are going to ask. Build them around the skills and qualities that are most important to the successful completion of the job's key tasks. Don't get caught wondering what you're going to say next.

Ask questions about the candidate's greatest accomplishments and what he or she learned from them. Then ask about his or her greatest failures or disappointments and what he or she learned from them. In both cases, you are seeking someone who views the past as a series of valuable learning experiences that have made him or her more capable of doing a better job in the future. Ask about the most important lesson the candidate has learned in his or her career up to now. These answers can be very revealing.

6

Look for the Best Predictor of Success

You can increase the quality and the longevity of the people you hire in a variety of great ways. One key method or insight can double your ability to hire and keep better people.

The one predictor of long-term job success that seems to be more powerful than any other single factor is called "self-selection." After thirty years of research into the career paths of many thousands of employees, experts found that an intense desire to work for their particular company, expressed during the initial job interviews, seemed to be common among most of the best managers and staff over the long term.

Self-selection takes place when a candidate, after interviewing with you and with other companies, concludes that he or she really wants to work for you and your company rather than anywhere else. If the candidate is qualified for the job, this is the best indicator you can get or create.

Here is a strategy you can use. After you have interviewed the candidate and decided that you would like to hire her, take some time to sell her on the job and the company. Tell her about the mission and values of the company, what you stand for and believe in. Explain to her why working there with you is a great career decision. Answer any questions she might have.

Then, bring the interview to a close. Encourage her to think about the job and then get back to you. Make no attempt to "close the sale."

When the candidate gets back to you and tells you that she really wants the job and wants to work for you, ask, "Why?"

"Why do you want to work here? Why would you want to work here rather than somewhere else?" Then remain silent and give the candidate a chance to answer.

Finally, ask her, "Specifically, how do you feel you could contribute to our company? Why should we hire you?"

The right candidate will have several answers to these questions. She will have given your offer a lot of thought and will be eager to get precisely *this* job. She will be positive and enthusiastic about the job possibility and will be eager to start. This is the very best attitude you could ask for in a job applicant.

Even if the job market is very tight, hire as patiently and as carefully as if you had all the candidates you could possibly ask for and all the time in the world. Once you have sold the person on wanting to work for you, you should have the person sell you on why she wants to work for you. This is the best single predictor of loyalty and long-term commitment that has yet been discovered.

Meanwhile, be cautious with anyone who is hesitant or reluctant about working for you. Be especially careful if a candidate plays "hard to get" or attempts to play you off against another prospective employer. A person whom you have to coax and tempt to take the job will often turn out to be disloyal. He or she will probably lack any long-term commitment to your organization.

◆

ACTION EXERCISES

Review your previous hires' attitudes, and even your own attitude when you took your current job. Note how often self-selection has gone hand in hand with good hiring decisions. Look for this attitude in every person you interview.

The next time you interview a job candidate, ask the person very early in the process why he or she would want to work for your company in the first place. This will either elicit a good answer or it will start the candidate thinking about it. The more excited the candidate is about the job, the better he or she will perform—from the very first day.

7

Probe Past Performance

Past performance is the only truly accurate predictor of future performance. It is the only measure that can be proven. All else is arguable, based on hope and conjecture and, often, exaggeration.

You may be hiring people right out of school. In that case, interview based on the sorts of things that they have done at school and during the summer to find out what kind of people they really are. Look at their nonwork experiences to see what qualities they have demonstrated that are essential to success in the job you are discussing.

In all other cases, past performance in the workplace is the very best indicator of what the candidate is likely to do in the job that you are offering. The rule is that you should hire based on *proven* past performance only.

Focus intensely on this one point. Proven successful experience that can be readily transferred to and duplicated in the job being discussed is so important in predicting job success that this one factor alone counts for more than any other single factor in making a good hiring decision.

When you hire a person, you are actually purchasing the ability of that person to achieve a specific result that is important to the success of your company. The accuracy with which you determine the ability of the candidate to deliver this result is the focal point of the hiring process.

Ask detailed questions about his or her previous work experiences and successes. Especially, ask about his or her greatest achievements in a previous job. Probe the answer you're given. Ask the candidate to elaborate and explain exactly what he or she did, what happened as a result, and how he or she felt about that accomplishment. What did he or she learn? Specifically, what did the candidate learn that he or she could apply to this job or to a future job?

Ask what kind of education, skills, or experiences he or she has had that qualifies him or her for the particular job you are offering. Like a detective, look for verifiable clues that can prove the candidate's ability to get the results you need. Listen carefully to the answers and probe by asking the questions, "What do you mean?" and "For example?" over and over.

Many people exaggerate their past accomplishments. They take credit for achievements that they were only partly responsible for. It is therefore essential that you ask them to describe the exact steps and process they went through to get the results claimed on their resumes.

Unless you are part of a large firm with lots of time and lots of money, do not expect to hire and place a new or inexperienced person in a key job. This is a high-risk policy. You are always better off looking for previous experience—and the more, the better.

ACTION EXERCISES

Clearly define the ideal job candidate in terms of the specific, applicable experiences he or she would have had that would virtually assure that he or she could get the results you need as quickly as possible.

Write out a list of various questions you could ask that would help you to determine that the candidate really knows how to do what you are looking for. Make notes during the interview. Ask follow-up questions to be sure. Assume nothing during this part of the interview.

Check Resumes and References Carefully

The most expensive mistakes you will ever make in hiring will be as a result of not properly checking and confirming the truth and validity of the hired person's background. An omission in this area can cost you thousands of dollars and many months of aggravation and frustration.

You will come across a special breed of job hunter in your career. These people are called "articulate incompetents." They seem to be everywhere. You must watch out for them.

These people have only one skill: the ability to interview well for a job. Beyond that, they are incapable of doing anything of value. They are extremely creative at making plausible excuses for nonperformance. They are usually charming and friendly, with good senses of humor. Everyone likes them, which is why you find yourself questioning your own judgment when they don't do the job you hired them for.

They are skillful in talking you out of checking their references. Often they will suggest that their previous bosses were jealous of their talents or dishonest in some way. They look so good that your desire to hire such an attractive personality can sometimes override your natural skepticism. This is where your insistence on reference checking can save you from making an expensive mistake.

The definition of management is "getting things done through others." Proper selection of those "others" upon whom your results depend determines 95 percent of your success as a manager. Proper selection is the key to building a great team. Checking resumes and references, making sure job candidates are exactly who they say they are, is therefore an essential part of a proper hiring process.

When you read a resume, look for simplicity and honesty. Look for a focus on accomplishments and achievements rather than a description of activities and length of time in a job. Look for "transferability of results." Look for someone who has already successfully done for someone else what you are hiring the new person to do for you.

Be skeptical about reference letters. They are often useless or deceptive. Sometimes they are given by a previous employer in exchange for the employee going in peace, rather than causing problems, when he or she has been separated from the company.

Here is a simple but effective strategy. Tell the candidate that your policy is to check references thoroughly. Ask, "Is there anything you would like to add before I call these people?" The information you get at this point can be quite revealing.

The way you check references is simple. Personally phone each person the candidate lists as a reference or who provides a reference letter. Introduce yourself and ask for the person's help. Explain that you are interviewing the candidate for a position, and explain the position. Promise confidentiality. Promise that you will not tell anyone about the answers you receive. Review what the candidate wrote about this previous job and corroborate that he or she did indeed perform the functions and accomplish the results claimed on the resume or application. Ask about the candidate's strengths. Then ask about any weaknesses that the candidate might have.

Many companies today will not tell you anything about a previous employee for fear of being sued. In this case, you can always ask this question: "Would you hire this person back again today if he applied for a job with you?" All this requires is a simple yes or no and is not an actionable response.

If the answer is yes, it is a good sign, one of the best you can get. If the person says no, this should be a red flag to you. At your next meeting with the candidate, or even by telephone, you should ask him why it is that his previous employer would not hire him back. Probe the answer carefully until you are clear. This can be critical for making the right decision. Generally speaking, a no answer is sufficient reason not to hire that particular person.

The last words you should use when checking a reference are these: "Thank you very much for your time. Before I go, is there anything else I should know about this person?" You should then remain completely silent and wait. Very often, a final, casual remark or insight that the person will give you just before hanging up will be invaluable in helping you make the right decision.

Once I checked the references of a woman I was interviewing. I got glowing praise from her previous employer about what a fine personality she had, how well she got along with others, and how likable she was. In response to my final question, "Is there anything else I should know?" her previous boss hesitated and then told me, "Well, she's got a big-company mentality. Bear that in mind."

Later, at great cost, I learned what he had been trying to tell me with the words "big-company mentality." She was an "articulate incompetent." She had no concern about the cost of anything. She was accustomed to working for a large company where the fact that she never got any results was covered up by the hustle and bustle of a large bureaucracy. In our small company setting, she proved to be a complete loss, incapable of completing even the simplest task. She incurred thousands of dollars in expenses that were complete wastes of money. It was an expensive hiring decision.

ACTION EXERCISES

Hire slowly and cautiously. Take the time to personally phone and check references with the exact person who supervised the candidate. Keep reminding yourself that fast hiring decisions are usually wrong hiring decisions. Listen carefully to the answers you get and be suspicious if something doesn't sound right.

Fully 54 percent of resumes and job applications are falsified in some way, especially in the areas of educational qualifications and actual job achievements. Take the time to verify every key detail that is vital to the successful performance of the job. Speak not only to previous employers but also to co-workers. Ask open-ended questions and listen closely to the answers. As William Shakespeare wrote, "Make haste slowly."

9

Practice the
Law of Three

Practicing the Law of Three is a powerful technique that can dramatically improve your accuracy in selecting the right people for you for the long term. Using the Law of Three, you interview at least three times for any position. With a little practice, you will learn to use this approach easily and automatically for the rest of your career.

You can use the Law of Three in several ways. The first application requires that you interview at least three candidates for any position. By speaking to three different people, you will get a much better sense of the kind of people who are available and what you really want. Never hire the first, or only, applicant you speak to. Following this practice can save you a lot of grief later.

Second, interview the candidate you like the most at least three times. A candidate who looks great at the first interview might look average at your second meeting and completely unacceptable at your third meeting. Hewlett-Packard insists on at least seven meetings and involves at least four different managers in the selection process. Other companies require as many as twenty-five meetings and interviews before they make a hiring decision. They know how important the hiring decision is to their long-term futures. Never make an employment offer until you have had a chance to see the person at least three times.

Never offer the job at the first interview. If you like a candidate, invite him or her back for a second and third interview. Remember, the best a candidate will ever appear will be at the first interview. At the second interview, you will see and experience a different person. At the third interview, the person may be so completely different that you will wonder what you were thinking when you interviewed him or her the first time.

Third, interview the person you like the most in at least three different locations. The first interview may be in your office. The second interview may be down the hall or in a separate room. The third interview can be across the street at a coffee shop. A person who looks good in your office may look average down the hall and completely mediocre when you take him out for coffee or lunch. A candidate on his best behavior begins to reveal his true temperament and personality when you talk to him in different locations.

Once I was offered a great job working as the personal assistant to the chairman of a large company. In the midst of our discussions, he suggested that we take a half-hour drive out of town to a farm he owned. Only after that drive and a stroll around the farm did he decide to hire me. I never forgot that experience.

Hiring decisions that you make solely by intuition or impulse can often turn out to be mistakes. Because humans are primarily emotional, we should deliberately create a separation or buffer between our emotional natures and our decisions. We can achieve this by slowing down the hiring process in the manner described above.

The fourth application of the Law of Three is to have the candidate interviewed by at least three other managers or potential coworkers. Don't rely solely on your own judgment in hiring someone. Get other people involved. Invite different perspectives. A person whom you may like initially may turn out to be completely unacceptable when other people have a chance to express their opinions.

In my company, everyone gets a chance to interview a new candidate, and then everyone votes on that candidate before he or she receives a job offer. It is absolutely amazing what information comes out when a candidate speaks to a potential coworker as opposed to a potential boss. My staff has unanimously rejected people who I thought looked and sounded terrific. Later, my staff turned out to be right.

A major advantage of having potential coworkers involved in the interview and hiring process is that if they like a candidate, the person will be off to a great start when he or she is hired. When coworkers feel that the hiring decision was influenced or determined by them, they feel a higher level of ownership and commitment to you, to the new person, and to the company. You get the double benefit of a better hiring decision and a more loyal and motivated workforce.

Since we began this multiple interview process, our turnover rate has dropped to almost zero, in a dynamic job market, even though we have an unemployment rate of less than 3 percent in our community.

The fifth application of the Law of Three is for you to interview at least three people who have worked with the candidate in the past. Follow up not only on the "sweetheart" references listed in the employment application, but also ask to speak to other people who have had direct personal experience with the candidate. Ask them for their opinions on the suitability of the person for the job under consideration.

Simply by slowing down the process of making a hiring decision, you will make fewer mistakes and better choices. By applying the many variations of the Law of Three to your hiring activities, you will dramatically increase your ability to hire and keep the best people.

ACTION EXERCISES

Create a cover sheet with checklists of the various "threes" that you can attach to the resume or application of each person you interview. Explain the Law of Three to the other people who work with you and ask them to help you use it to improve the quality of each hiring decision.

The next time you interview an attractive candidate for a position, discipline yourself to apply the Law of Three to this process from beginning to end. Afterward, analyze and discuss with your colleagues and co-workers how this process worked. Many managers and executives have told me that this simple system is one of the most valuable business techniques they ever learned.

10

Make the Decision Properly

Proper decision making is a key management skill. This is where you demonstrate your ability to choose your staff and set the tone for your employees' tenure with the company. You must conduct this part of the process with care and professionalism.

Before you make a final hiring decision, take some time to review what you know about the candidate and the company. First of all, consider the corporate climate and the people mix in your company. This will play a vital part in the new employee's future performance. Will he or she fit into your corporate culture and climate? Will he or she be happy in your type of business? These considerations are very important.

Use the "family member" method of selection. Ask yourself, "Would I feel comfortable inviting this person to my home to have dinner with my family on Sunday night?" This is a great question to ask because it gives you a better intuitive sense for whether or not this person will fit in with you and the other people on your team.

Would you want your son or daughter to work with this person or for this person? If not, why not? When you consider assigning one of your children to work under this person, it gives you a much clearer picture of whether or not this person is appropriate for your business for the long term.

Do you genuinely like this person? Be perfectly selfish. You should hire only people whom you like and enjoy. After all, you are inviting someone to join your "business family." Think long term. Would you be comfortable working with this person for the next ten or twenty years? Remember that long-term thinking dramatically improves short-term decision making.

Finally, review your thoughts and feelings with other people who will be working with this person. Ask for their insights and opinions. Listen to them carefully. Then, take some time by yourself to decide whether or not this is the right person for you.

Ask yourself, "What would happen if I didn't hire this person at all? How much of a difference would it make? Is there any urgency?"

Harvey Mackay tells about going through a six-month hiring process to find a new salesman. He interviewed thirty-five candidates, many of them several times. At the end of the process, he decided not to hire any of them. After years of experience, he had learned that a bad hiring decision is worse than no hiring decision at all.

◆

ACTION EXERCISES

The time for you to make the proper hiring decision is at the end of the interview process and before you finalize your choice. This is when you need to give the situation a good deal of thought. Go slow. Take your time. Listen to your intuition and trust your instincts, but also check the facts.

When in doubt about hiring someone, there is usually a good reason. Delay the decision. Gather more information. Talk to more people. Talk to the candidate again. Proceed only when you are convinced that this person is the right choice. You will save yourself a lot of problems later.

11

Negotiate the Right Salary

Money is a very emotional issue for most people. The way you determine what you are going to pay the chosen candidate and the benefits you are going to offer sets the stage for discussions and decisions about remuneration for the months and years ahead. You must handle this issue with care.

Here is a good rule to follow with regard to salary, bonuses, and other forms of income: "Good people are free."

Good people are *free* in that they contribute more in dollar value than you pay them in salary and bonuses. Every good person that you add to your payroll increases your bottom line. The profitability of your company is largely determined by your ability to attract and keep good people who put in more than they take out. For this reason, the amount you pay should largely be determined by the potential contribution of the employee, not some arbitrary rules in the marketplace or in your industry.

The fact is that today you have to pay talented people whatever it takes to hire them in comparison with what they could get working somewhere else. At the same time, you are buying a service for your company and you are duty bound to purchase this quantity and quality of service at the very best price. Therefore, the better prepared you are for a salary negotiation, the better deal you will make.

First, do your homework. Ask around to determine what the job is worth in the current market. Phone personnel or placement agencies and find out how much it would cost to hire a person with this particular level of skill. Read the want ads in the newspaper. Consider how much you are currently paying to people in similar positions.

Second, think through and determine how much you can afford to pay for someone in this position. But remember that whatever the market is paying is the *minimum* that you will have to pay as well. People may not be motivated solely by money, but money is a key consideration when it comes to taking a job. People will not accept less from one company than they can get from another for the same job.

If you are hiring someone away from another company, you will have to pay at least 10 percent more than he or she is currently receiving. Ten percent seems to be the psychological point at which people will consider moving from one company to another. This is especially true for younger workers with shallow loyalties to their current employers.

If you are unsure about how much to offer, ask the candidate, "What sort of salary or remuneration are you looking for?" or "What do you feel this position is worth?" Listen carefully to the answer. Neither agree nor disagree. Simply ask, "How did you arrive at that amount?" And listen again.

You can also ask, "How much money would you have to make to feel comfortable in this job?" Most people have two numbers in mind when they are negotiating compensation. The first is the amount that they would ideally *like* to make, which is usually far above what they've ever made before. The other, more accurate, number is the amount that they actually expect to make, the amount that they would be satisfied with. Your job is to discover the second number.

An important part of the total pay package is the range of benefits you are offering as part of the job. An attractive medical insurance package can be more valuable to a person with a family than a higher salary. Flexible work hours, a company car, or generous vacation periods can offset a lower starting wage. Be sure to emphasize these points in your negotiation.

If possible, start the person at a lower wage than she requests, but agree to increase her salary within ninety days if she does a great job. Specify that this first ninety days will be her probation or trial period.

At the end of ninety days, sit down and review the job to determine how well things are going. At that point, assuming that you both are happy, you will discuss an increase.

None of these suggestions, however, are engraved in stone. Because people and performance can be so varied and unpredictable, every recommendation in this book is subject to revision in the face of new information. For example, I hired a controller once at a salary below what she was asking, with the agreement that we would review it in ninety days. She started on a Monday, and I increased her salary on Tuesday because she was obviously so competent at her job. I never regretted it.

Don't be afraid to pay well for talented people. Remember, you always get what you pay for, especially in today's job market.

◆

ACTION EXERCISES

Review your current salary and compensation structure to be sure that it is in alignment with the existing job market. With the valuable people you already have whom you cannot afford to lose, consider giving them an increase as an insurance policy against their being hired away. Offer them additional benefits, especially if competitors are offering them.

Be open to the possibility that you may have to offer more than you intended to get a qualified person to take the job. Your goal is to pay exactly the right amount and no more. Therefore, do your homework so that you have a clear picture of what the job pays in today's market.

12

Start Them Off Right

The time and attention you invest in a new hire at the beginning will give you a tremendous payoff in improved productivity and performance in the weeks and months ahead.

Good people are too valuable and scarce today for the old "sink or swim" method of hiring and starting new employees. To ramp up quickly and get right into their new jobs, employees require a "hands-on" approach from the first day. The way you start new employees can have a measurable impact on their performance and effectiveness for many years.

On day one, take some time to explain to the new employee the values, the vision, the mission, and the purpose of the company. Explain why and how your products and services really make a difference in the lives and work of your customers and your clients. Sell the new employee on the importance and value of his job and explain how it fits in with the activities of the company. Help the new person understand how valuable and important he is in the big picture.

Have his work area prepared and organized. If possible, have his business cards printed and ready. Make him feel at home immediately.

Introduce the new employee to his coworkers on the first day. Familiarize him with the company and how it functions. Many companies actually have a one- or two-week orientation program for new employees to cover all the items just mentioned. At the very least, spend time with the employee on his first day so that he feels welcomed into his new family. This process is much easier if the new person has already met with one or more of his peers during the interview process.

Create a "buddy system" for each new person. If you cannot personally orient the new hire, assign another capable person to work with the new hire as a buddy or friend. This friend can show the new person around and answer any questions.

When you start people off right, they will be far more positive, motivated, and committed to their jobs and to the company. The first few days and weeks are extremely important in creating the proper attitudes in the mind of the new employee.

◆

ACTION EXERCISES

When your new employee arrives at work on his first day, meet with him and tell him that you are happy to have him working there. Tell him that he has made a good choice. Offer to help him in any way possible. Tell him that your door is always open if he has any questions. Act like a host welcoming someone into your home.

Assign the new person to someone who will be responsible for showing him the ropes. On the morning of the first day of work, sit down with both people, introduce them to each other, tell them what they will be doing together, and answer any questions.

13

Start Them Off Strong

I f you have made the right selection, the new person will be ready, willing, and eager to start her new job. Psychologically, she will be looking forward to doing something productive and becoming both useful and important as quickly as possible. What you do on the first day will have an effect on her attitude for many weeks and months into the future.

The key is to start her off with lots of work to do. People love to be busy and never so much as when they are nervous and unsure at the beginning of a new job. A full workload from the first day makes the job challenging and exciting.

As you hand out the assignments, provide lots of opportunity for feedback and discussion about the work. When people have ample opportunity to ask questions and talk about the job, they identify themselves with the company much more rapidly. They become far more motivated and committed to doing a good job than if they are started off slowly or if they receive limited feedback.

Be prepared to take the time necessary to teach the new person how to do her new job. No matter how competent or well meaning she is, she will need guidance and instruction to do the job properly. This direction is a key responsibility of management.

As soon as you possibly can, compliment the new person on an idea, suggestion, or accomplishment. Find an opportunity to catch her doing something right. Meet with the person, talk to her, and give her praise and encouragement at every opportunity, especially during the earlier stages. You cannot be too supportive or reassuring during this critical time for the new employee.

People are hypersensitive during the first days and weeks of a new job and are most open to positive influence at this time. Make sure that these are bright, shining moments for your new employee so that she feels genuinely happy about working for you and with you.

◆

ACTION EXERCISES

Make a list of tasks for the new person and review it together on the morning of the first day. Treat the new employee like a valuable and productive team member from the beginning. Aim to create a workload that keeps the new person going at full capacity from the first day.

Work closely with the new person during the first days and weeks, or have someone else work closely with him or her. Give regular and timely feedback on the work. Expect the new employee to make mistakes and to be unsure and unclear about the job for the first few days and even weeks. Be patient and supportive during this learning period.

14

Solve Problems Quickly

We are living in a world of incredible change and turbulence. Because each person is different from every other person, misunderstandings can and will take place all the time. Personality and performance problems can arise even among the very best and most capable of people. Often these misunderstandings and problems are not the fault of the employee at all.

When a problem of any kind arises, deal with it *immediately.* Many problems are temporary and passing. They are caused by external events and they blow over quickly. When something goes wrong, you should call the person into your office or go and see him or her as soon as possible. Deal with the difficulty promptly, whatever it is.

Expect there to be a reasonable explanation for everything. Resist the temptation to blame, accuse, or pass judgment before you gather sufficient information. Instead, be empathetic and supportive. Rather than accusing or complaining, ask questions to find out exactly what has happened and why. Then, listen patiently to the answers.

Remember, many employment problems are the fault of the company or the supervisor. The fact is that nobody does something deliberately that he or she feels is wrong. Everyone wants to do a good job. Everyone wants to be seen as a valuable person and to be respected by his or her boss and coworkers.

Two key problems cause most difficulties in the workplace. Both of these are the fault of managers. They are (1) lack of direction and (2) lack of feedback.

Where clear, specific, time-bounded direction is lacking, your employee will not be certain what you want and expect. Without clear instructions or standards of performance to guide behavior, you cannot expect excellent or timely performance of a task. This is a major cause of inefficiency and mistakes in the workplace.

Without clear direction, the individual will probably do the very best that he or she possibly can, but it might be the wrong task in the wrong way and in the wrong order of priority. Even a talented and dedicated person will perform poorly if he or she is not certain what it is you really want.

When people start and complete a task, especially an important task, they experience a sense of closure, the pleasure of completion. This act of finishing a task raises their self-esteem, increases their self-respect, and improves their self-confidence. They feel like *winners*. The opposite of this success experience is the feeling of confusion and inadequacy that accompanies work on unclear tasks or objectives. This *losing* feeling is often exacerbated by disapproval and criticism from a disgruntled boss, who is probably responsible for the misunderstanding in the first place. This is why the biggest single demotivator in the world of work is not knowing what's expected.

The good news is that the most powerful single motivator in the world of work is being told exactly what one is expected to do. When people are absolutely clear about what the boss wants, and when and to what standard, they feel more competent and confident. They feel more focused and directed. They feel more in control of themselves and their work. And these feelings are largely determined by the boss.

Lack of feedback on performance is the second major source of demotivation and dissatisfaction in the workplace. People need to know, on a regular basis, how well they are doing. If they are making a mistake, they need this pointed out to them. If they are doing the job right, they need to have this reaffirmed and recognized. Providing this steady stream of feedback is a chief responsibility of an effective executive. You cannot expect people to remain motivated and enthused about their work if they never hear anything from you about how well they are doing it.

Miscommunication or lack of communication of some kind causes probably 95 percent of problems within organizations. A superior manager always assumes that he or she is at fault when an employee fails to perform to an expected standard. When you start from that point of view, you will solve most of your performance problems quickly and easily. You will be back in control.

ACTION EXERCISES

See yourself as a professional problem solver, no matter what your official title. Expect your work life to be a continuous, never-ending series of problems. Learn to welcome them as a validation of your worth. In fact, if there were no problems for you to solve, your job could be automated or turned over to a junior person.

Focus on the solution rather than the problem for the rest of your career. When there is a difficulty, ask, "What's the solution? What do we do now? What's the next step?" Focus on the future rather than the past. Focus on what can be done rather than who is to blame. Then get busy solving the problem and achieving your business goals.

15

Improve Performance Professionally

Job descriptions and job requirements change so rapidly that you must continually redefine them for each employee. Here are five simple steps that you can use on a regular basis to improve the performance of every person who reports to you.

First, sit down with each employee and explain clearly what he or she is expected to do. Take your time. Describe the results that you want from the job. Make the results clear and objective. If the job is important enough, write out what you discuss so that the employee can read it and take it away with him or her.

Second, set measurable standards of performance for the job you want done. Quantify everything. Put financial measures on every single output responsibility, if possible. Find a way to measure the different aspects of the performance of the job. One of the great rules in management is "What gets measured gets done." Another is "If you can't measure it, you can't manage it."

Third, never *assume* understanding. When you have delegated an assignment, ask the employee to repeat it back to you in his or her own words. Never meet with a staff member to give an assignment without insisting that the staff member have a pad of paper on which he or she can write down what you say.

In fully 50 percent of cases, when the employee reads back what you have just said, he or she will have misunderstood your instructions in some way. This is the time to catch the error, not later.

Fourth, give regular feedback on performance. As Ken Blanchard says, "Feedback is the breakfast of champions."

To do their very best, people need regular feedback to tell them that they are on track or off track. They need to know when they are doing well and when they can do better. And the newer a person is at a job, the more and regular feedback they require in order to do the job well.

Fifth, inspect what you expect. Delegation is not abdication. When you delegate a job, you assign responsibility but you still remain accountable. If the job is important, inspect the job and assess progress on a regular basis. Not only does this impress upon the employee the importance of the job, but it also gives you an opportunity to get regular feedback and catch mistakes early in the process where the cost can be considerably less than later on.

People love the feeling of doing their jobs and doing them well. They love the feeling of success and contribution. Especially, people love to get positive feedback and recognition for having done a good job. Your job is to satisfy this basic need of all the people who look to you for leadership.

ACTION EXERCISES

Take the time to think through and explain each job to each employee. Clarity at this point enables the employee to perform better and with less supervision. It increases productivity and saves you a considerable amount of time.

Accept complete responsibility for any task that you delegate. Stay on top of it, and the more important it is, the closer you should monitor it. Your job is to get the work done through others, and this is the best way to do it.

16

Assume the Best of Intentions

Misunderstandings, conflict, and friction are normal and natural elements of the human condition, especially when very different people, with extremely complex lives, are working together for many hours in a small space, like an office environment. How you deal with and resolve these inevitable and unavoidable problems of daily work life is a key measure of your intelligence, your maturity, and your skill as a manager.

No matter what happens or how it appears initially, always assume that the other person is doing the very best he can with what he has available to him. When difficulties arise in an employee's work or in a relationship in the office, always assume the best of intentions. Always assume that he means well. Resist the temptation to become angry, impatient, or judgmental.

One of my personal rules for living is never to allow myself to become *stressed out* because of my dissatisfaction with the performance or behavior of someone who reports to me. To minimize this type of stress, you should deal with problems and misunderstandings as they arise. You should never go home with a problem left unresolved or a difficulty that you have not confronted and dealt with in some way. Here is how you do it:

First, take the problem employee aside and discuss the problem in private, with the door closed. Never criticize or correct someone in the presence of others. Behind closed doors, explain clearly that you feel there is a problem that should be dealt with. Tell the employee that you want to discuss it and find a solution. Do this without accusation or attack.

Second, be specific about the problem or misunderstanding. Give concrete examples of why you are concerned. The more specific you can be, the more accurate and helpful can be the responses of the employee.

Third, hear the employee out completely. Listen carefully to his side of the problem. The Law of the Situation says that every problem concerning any two or more people is unique; each situation requires different rules and decisions to deal with it. You will often find that the employee's definition of the problem or explanation of what happened throws an entirely new light on the situation.

Fourth, if the employee is at fault in some way, discuss and agree on how his performance is to change and by how much. People cannot hit a target that they cannot see. When you point out exactly what needs to be done to resolve a problem, people will then know exactly what they have to do to get back on track. They will be grateful to you for the way you are handling the situation. Remember, people cannot resolve every problem by themselves. They sometimes need help.

Fifth, monitor and follow up on what was agreed to in the discussion. Give feedback and additional help whenever necessary. Be supportive and helpful. Sometimes a problem employee can be turned into a superstar employee under the right manager.

Finally, keep accurate notes and records of the discussion. If you suspect that this problem may be the tip of an iceberg that can lead to the severance of the employee, protect yourself by keeping a written record of the discussion, when and why it took place, and what was agreed upon as a solution. This can save you an enormous amount of trouble later.

◆

ACTION EXERCISES

Expect to have difficulties and challenges with employees as a natural and unavoidable part of the job. Decide in advance to assume that each person is doing the best he or she can and that any problem can be resolved if you approach it in the right spirit.

Identify a problem situation that exists in your workplace today. Take the involved parties aside, behind closed doors, and explain to them that you want a resolution. Serve as a mediator until a solution is agreed upon. Aim to maintain harmony in your workplace at all times.

17

Satisfy Their Deepest Needs

G ood people are harder to find today, and harder to please, than ever before. One of your key responsibilities as a manager is to create an environment, physical and emotional, where people feel safe, secure, valuable, and respected. Your job as a manager is to create a great place to work.

To keep the very best people, you need to satisfy their emotional needs as well as their financial and physical needs. Each person has three major emotional needs in the world of work. These are for dependence, independence, and interdependence.

Dependence needs deal with the desire that everyone has to be part of something bigger than himself or herself. People want to belong to an organization or support a cause. They want to feel that what they are doing makes a difference in the world. People want the security, comfort, and satisfaction of being protected under the umbrella of a company or greater authority. They want to work with and for a boss that they can look up to, trust, and respect.

You can satisfy this dependency need by continually reminding people of the corporate mission and vision. Tell them why the company exists, what you stand for and believe in, and the difference your products and services make in the lives of your customers. Increased loyalty and commitment are the result of your satisfying this basic dependency need.

Each person has needs for *independence* as well. This is the need to stand out from the crowd, to be recognized as a special and important person in the eyes of others. This is the need to be recognized and appreciated for one's own personal qualities and accomplishments. Whenever you say or do anything that makes a person feel more valuable, you satisfy the need for independence and the feeling of importance that goes with it.

The third type of need that each person has is for *interdependence,* to be part of a team, to work effectively and cooperatively with others. Human beings are social animals, and they are happy only when they are working with other people in a harmonious and productive environment. The very best companies and the very best managers are always looking for ways to create a greater sense of happiness and cooperation among their people. This is a chief role of management and leadership.

The way you satisfy all three needs—for dependence, independence, and interdependence—is by listening carefully, responding appropriately, and remaining flexible in your dealings with each person. Recognize that each person has needs that make him or her different from every other person. Your job is to be aware of these differences and to respond to them in the most appropriate way.

ACTION EXERCISES

Take some time each day to remind people about the importance of what you are doing as a company and what they are doing as individuals. Perhaps the most powerful tool to satisfy dependence needs is for you to tell stories about and read letters from happy customers and tell people how they are instrumental in creating or generating these responses.

Plan regular occasions where the staff can gather informally to socialize and get to know each other better. The more people interact with each other, the more they will feel part of something bigger than themselves, and the more they will enjoy their work.

18

Practice Participatory Management

According to experts, the average employed person today works at less than 50 percent of capacity. According to some studies, fully 55 percent of employees today are "not engaged" with their work. They are merely going through the motions and doing just enough to avoid being laid off or fired.

One of the most valuable contributions you can make to your organization is to create an environment where people enjoy working and feel motivated to perform at higher and higher levels. Participatory management is one of the most effective tools you can use for achieving this goal.

In the old paradigm, employees were supposed to be grateful that they had a job. They went to work and they did what was expected of them. Then they went home. Today, however, the situation is different. Employees want to be fully involved in their work. In fact, "being in the know" is considered one of the major sources of job satisfaction, ranking ahead of pay and benefits in many employee surveys.

There is no better way to build a powerful, positive team of highly motivated people than by bringing them together on a regular basis to talk, discuss, argue, work out problems, make plans, and generally share information, ideas, and experiences. This is the key to building peak-performance teams and company spirit.

One of my clients, the president of a large distribution company, told me that his business had been losing money for two years and was on the verge of going broke. Then he attended one of my programs and learned about the importance of weekly meetings among the staff at all levels. His company had not held regular meetings for years, so he decided to give it a try.

When he called his managers together for the first weekly meeting, they were extremely suspicious. They sat with their arms folded and contributed little. But after two or three weeks of open meetings, the barriers began to come down. The managers began making suggestions to increase sales, cut costs, and improve profits. Within six months, the entire company had turned around.

Each manager began holding meetings with his or her staff every week as well. The psychological climate in the company went from one of fear and distrust to one of openness and high energy in a very short period of time. Losses turned to profits and the company began to grow again. My client told me that weekly meetings had saved his company from bankruptcy.

You should hold a general staff meeting at least once each week with all the people who report directly to you. At this meeting, every person should be listed on the agenda as an agenda item. Every person should be encouraged to give a brief report on what he or she is doing, how it is working, what suggestions he or she has, and what assistance or resources he or she might require. Everyone discusses the work and shares with the others any problems and frustrations. The manager takes notes and, wherever possible, takes action on the decisions made by the group.

You will be absolutely amazed at how quickly these regular meetings build stronger bonds of friendship and cooperation among your staff. All kinds of problems are ironed out quickly. People begin to share their own personal experiences. And best of all, they begin to laugh together and see themselves as important parts of a team and of the company as a whole.

The more you involve your staff, at every level and in every decision, the more motivated and enthusiastic they will become to carry out the decisions and to achieve the goals that you agree upon. Participatory management is one of the fastest acting and most successful management techniques you can use to build a high-performance team.

ACTION EXERCISES

Call your staff together for the first of your weekly meetings. List every person on the agenda. Go around the room and ask each person to tell the group what he or she is working on, how it is going, and what help he or she might require.

Rotate the chairmanship of the meeting each week among the staff. Give each person a turn to run the meeting while you participate as a regular staff member. You will be delighted to see how quickly people light up and get involved when they are invited to participate.

19

Make Them Feel Important

Imagine that every person in your company is wearing a sign around his or her neck, all day long, that says "Make me feel important."

In every interaction with every single person, you should respond to this basic human request. You should always be looking for ways to make people feel important and valuable as parts of your team.

You can practice four key behaviors every day to raise people's self-esteem and make them feel more important and valuable. They all begin with the letter *A*.

The first *A* stands for *appreciation*. Take every opportunity to thank each person for everything that she does, small or large, in carrying out her duties. Every time you say "thank you" to a person, her self-esteem goes up. She feels better and more valuable. And she becomes even more motivated to do more of the things for which she received appreciation in the first place. A boss with an "attitude of gratitude" is one of the most effective leaders in any organization.

The second A stands for *approval*. Give praise and approval on every occasion, for every accomplishment of whatever size. Give praise for every good effort. Give praise for every good suggestion or idea. Especially, praise people when they do something that goes above and beyond the call of duty.

Praise immediately, right after the event. Praise specifically. Praise regularly. Whenever you praise another person, she experiences it physically and emotionally. Her self-esteem goes up and she feels happier about herself and her job. The good news is that whatever you praise gets repeated. People will do more and more of those things that are the most approved of by people whose opinions they value.

The third A stands for *admiration*. As Abraham Lincoln said, "Everybody likes a compliment." Regularly compliment people on their personal traits and qualities, such as punctuality and persistence. Compliment them on their possessions, such as their clothes, their cars, and their accessories. Compliment them on their achievements, both at work and in their private lives.

Every time you express admiration to another person, especially in front of others, you raise that person's self-esteem. You cause her to like herself more and make her feel better and more committed to you and the company.

The final *A*, perhaps the most important of all, is the behavior of *attention*. Paying attention means that you listen to your staff when they want to talk to you. Listen patiently. Listen attentively. Listen quietly. Listen calmly. Listen thoughtfully. Listen without interrupting.

Whenever a person is attentively listened to by someone she respects, her self-esteem goes up. She feels more important and valuable. She feels more committed to both the person and the job. She feels better about herself and does her job better.

Remember, you do not have to act on the ideas or suggestions of people when they talk to you. You just have to listen carefully, nod, smile, and thank them for their input. People get tremendous satisfaction from having an opportunity to express themselves honestly to their bosses. Your job is just to listen.

◆

ACTION EXERCISES

Take a walk through your office and stop to say something nice to each person. Praise, recognition, and thanks expressed by a senior person have a powerful impact on how a person feels about himself or herself. Do this regularly.

Each day, select at least one of your staff and praise him or her in front of someone else. Make a big deal of it. Praise received in public makes a person feel more important and appreciated than anything else you can do or say.

20

Create a Great Place to Work

Employee retention is vital to business success in our current job market. The high costs of employee turnover can be enough, all by themselves, to put a company under water.

When you have hired, trained, and developed a team of top people, you must do everything possible to, as Shakespeare said, "Bind them to you with hoops of steel." Once you get them, you should never lose them, except by your own choice or decision. You must create a great place to work, and the first way to do that is, as W. Edwards Deming said, "Drive out fear."

Your job is to create a high-trust environment where people feel terrific about themselves. They feel positive and happy. They feel protected and secure. They feel comfortable in your presence.

The way that you create these conditions is by refusing to criticize, condemn, or complain about anything. Do not blame other people for making mistakes or for doing things wrong. Instead, create an environment where the fears of failure and rejection that hold most people back are simply eliminated from the workplace.

The key to building a high-trust environment is for you to allow people to make honest mistakes without criticizing them or making them feel bad or deficient in any way. When people feel that they have permission to take risks and make mistakes, without any fear of retribution, they will feel more confident and secure. As a result, they will be more thoughtful and creative in achieving the company's goals. They will perform at their best.

Whenever someone does something that doesn't work out or makes a mistake, and this will happen regularly, instead of criticizing, focus on the solution, on what can be done. Help the person to identify the valuable lesson or lessons contained in this experience. Help the person to grow in skill and wisdom from the mistake. Acknowledge the problem and then ask, "What did you learn? The next time this comes up, why don't we do it this way?"

Help people to learn and to grow from temporary failures and setbacks. Encourage them to learn everything they can from every mistake. Whenever possible, give them praise and acknowledgment for having taken a risk in the first place.

A famous story is told about Thomas J. Watson Sr., the founder of IBM, who one day called a young vice president into his office to review his work. The young executive had just spent ten million dollars on a research project that had failed completely. When the young vice president arrived, he offered his resignation to Watson, saying, "You don't have to fire me. I'll go peacefully. I know I've made a mistake." Watson replied, "Fire you? Why would I fire you? I've just spent ten million dollars on your education. Now, let's talk about your next assignment." This is the behavior of a great executive.

The only way people can learn and grow and develop in judgment and wisdom is by trying things and making mistakes. Your job is to make sure that every lesson learned can be applied to making your company even more successful in the future. This is the chief way that you make your company a great place to work.

The second way to create a great place to work is by structuring jobs in such a way that they are responsive to the most pressing needs of your employees, especially in the area of flexible hours. This issue alone is one of the most important of all considerations for many people working today.

The majority of employees have family responsibilities of some kind involving children or aged parents. When a problem or emergency arises in the family, employees should know that they can take time off from work to respond to the need quickly. This support and understanding from the boss and the company can be more important than any other factor in assuring employee happiness and a long-term commitment to the company.

Some years ago, as a parent with young children, I noticed that most of my staff had young children as well. Some were single parents, trying to juggle the twin responsibilities of work and home, including child raising, school attendance, doctor's visits, unexpected illnesses, and emergencies. This caused an enormous amount of stress on the parents who were affected.

I decided to introduce a policy to my company called "Families Come First." I called everyone together and announced that, from that day forward, if ever anyone had a family need, especially involving children, it would take precedence over anything else.

What this meant in practice was that the employee dealing with a family problem was free to leave work during the day or come in late or leave early or not come in to work at all, solely based on his or her own personal judgment. There would be no docking of pay and no overtime requirement to make up for the time lost.

We subsequently extended this policy to paying our people when they were off work to have babies, to have surgery, to recover at home, and even to attend funerals or handle family crises where they would have to be gone for several days. Our "Families

Come First" policy has cost us many thousands of dollars and has been perhaps the best personnel policy we have ever introduced. No one takes advantage of it, and all employees appreciate knowing that they have the flexibility and freedom to come and go according to their own and their families' needs.

Our people are valuable and precious to us. Their personal lives and feelings are important. To demonstrate our belief in these principles, we put our money where our mouths are. As a result of this policy, and of practicing the other ideas described in this book, we have created a happy, harmonious team of positive, productive people who like themselves, like each other, and do terrific work, virtually without supervision. And so can you.

◆

ACTION EXERCISES

See yourself as a teacher, guide, and counselor to your staff. Take every opportunity to help them grow by walking them through their mistakes and encouraging them to identify the lessons they have learned that they can apply in the future.

Discipline yourself to look for the good in every difficult situation. Find one or more lessons that you can learn from every setback. Imagine that every problem has been sent to you at exactly the right time to teach you something you need to know to be more successful in the future. Never stop searching until you find it.

Introduce flexible work hours and a family-friendly policy among your staff. Give people more freedom and more responsibility at the same time. You'll be happily amazed at how well they respond.

Focus on Your People Continually

This is perhaps the most important managerial success principle of all. If you focus on your people, your people will focus on the business and on making it a success. If you focus your energies on making people feel great about themselves, you will bring out of them the highest levels of creativity, positive energy, cooperation, commitment, and dedication to getting the job done and getting it done well.

It is said that there are never any bad soldiers under a good general. The fact is that morale does not rise in an organization; it filters down from the top. You are the one who sets the tone for the people who report to you. You are the spark plug, the quarterback, and the key factor in the productivity of your entire company or department. As the leader, you are the person who is more responsible than anyone else when it comes to hiring and keeping the best people and then shaping them into a high-performance team that gets great results week after week, month after month.

In today's job market, you should treat each person as though he or she were a *volunteer.* Imagine that you are running a nonprofit organization or a political campaign. Imagine that everyone who comes to work for you is a volunteer who is giving up personal time that he or she could just as easily spend somewhere else.

Because so many jobs are available today, each person who works for you is, in effect, a volunteer. Each person can go somewhere else. Each person who works for you has lots of other opportunities. And the more competent your employees, the more opportunities they have. The more valuable they are to your company, the easier it is for them to go somewhere else if they are not happy where they are.

When you treat each person like a volunteer and continually express your appreciation to him or her for working with you and helping you to achieve your goals, your attitude will be more positive and considerate. You will be far more polite and courteous to each person. You will be more supportive and encouraging. You will be friendlier and more sympathetic. You will not criticize, complain, or get angry when things go wrong. After all, you may remind yourself, these people are volunteers and they can leave at any time if they are not happy.

ACTION EXERCISES

Continually imagine what it would be like to lose your key people. Act as if they were considering other job offers already. Treat them as you would if they were critical to the functioning of your company—because they are.

Take whatever steps are necessary to assure harmony and a general feeling of goodwill at work. Commit to creating an environment where people are happy to come to work and reluctant to leave. Think every day about what you can do to improve the climate at work.

Conclusion:
Putting It All Together

At every stage of economic and business development, different skills and abilities are necessary to survive and thrive. At one time, you had to be focused and determined to do your job well. You had to constantly outperform the competition. You had to make sure that everybody around you thought and behaved the same way. These qualities are still essential, but in addition, there is another skill you must have.

Today, the most important skill you can develop is the ability to hire and keep the best people. Your ability to do this will have a greater impact on your success and income than perhaps any other single skill you can acquire.

Here are the twenty-one great ideas you can use to achieve this goal:

1. **Make Selection Your Top Priority**—Take the time to select new people carefully, realizing that perhaps 95 percent of your success as a manager will be determined by the people you choose to work with you.

2. **Think Through the Job**—Stand back and look at the job objectively. Determine the results required from the position, the skills necessary to get those results, and the personality attributes of the ideal candidate.

3. **Write Out the Job Description**—Think on paper! Take a few minutes to write out a description of the ideal person you would like to hire to fill a particular position. List the qualities and skills you are seeking according to their importance. Refer to this description regularly.

4. **Cast a Wide Net**—Put the law of probabilities to work in your favor. Seek ideal job candidates everywhere, among your staff, friends, and personal contacts and through both placement agencies and Internet/newspaper advertising. Contact community colleges and local universities. Search continually for the people you need.

5. **Interview Effectively**—Prepare thoroughly for each employment interview by writing out your key questions in advance. Probe for information on past performance, current ambitions, and future goals. Don't start selling until you've decided to buy.

6. **Look for the Best Predictor of Success**—Interview, ask questions, and be alert to a candidate who really wants to work for you and your company. This attitude alone does not assure success, but it is the

best indication that the candidate is going to do well in the job.

7. **Probe Past Performance**—Successful experience is the focal point of the interviewing process. You are hiring a person who can contribute a specific result to your business, and the only assurance of future performance is proven past performance.

8. **Check Resumes and References Carefully**—Be sure to verify every detail that a candidate gives you about his or her past. Most resumes are falsified in some way. Take the time to check and double-check that the person has the experience to do the job properly.

9. **Practice the Law of Three**—Slow down and improve the hiring process by meeting with the candidate three times before making a decision. Interview the candidate in three places. Have the candidate interview with three staff members. Interview three references. Take your time in the beginning to save time later.

10. **Make the Decision Properly**—The true test of an excellent executive is his or her ability to make this key decision correctly. Once you have gathered all the information and checked the candidate's references, you should listen to your "inner voice" and trust your personal judgment.

11. **Negotiate the Right Salary**—Take your time to mutually agree upon the correct amount that you will have to pay to hire the right person. This is an important and emotional period of the hiring process and sets the stage for salary negotiations in the future.

12. **Start Them Off Right**—The first day and week of a new job sets the stage in the employee's mind for the months and years to come. Take your time and make sure that the new person feels welcome and at ease in the new job.

13. **Start Them Off Strong**—Prepare a complete work plan for the new person and give him or her lots to do from the first hour of the first day. People love to be busy, and how busy they are required to be on the first day determines how busy they will be in the future.

14. **Solve Problems Quickly**—Move quickly to solve problems and clear up misunderstandings. See yourself as a professional problem solver, no matter what your title may be. Always focus on the future and what can be done rather than the past and who might be to blame.

15. **Improve Performance Professionally**—Your job as a manager is to accept complete responsibility for getting results through others. Take the time to delegate clearly and supervise effectively to assure the very best work, on time and on budget.

16. **Assume the Best of Intentions**—People problems are inevitable, unavoidable, and continuous at work. Nonetheless, everyone is trying to do his or her best, and your attitude should reflect this basic belief.

17. **Satisfy Their Deepest Needs**—Work every day to create an environment where each person's needs for dependence, independence, and interdependence can be satisfied in the pursuit of company goals.

18. **Practice Participatory Management**—Bring your staff together for regular meetings to discuss the work and share ideas. Keep everyone involved in the process. This is the only way to build a great team.

19. **Make Them Feel Important**—The more people like themselves, the more motivated they are to do a good job and the happier they are at work. Take every opportunity to build them up and make them feel good about themselves.

20. **Create a Great Place to Work**—Build trust, confidence, and security by allowing honest mistakes without criticizing, complaining, or threatening the person with demotion or punishment. Allow flexibility in how and when people do their jobs.

21. **Focus on Your People Continually**—Your staff members are the only irreplaceable elements in your business. Treat them as if they were volunteers, with

lots of options available to them, and they work for you only because you treat them so well.

It has been said that all of life is the study of attention. Where your attention goes, your life goes as well. When you begin to pay greater attention to hiring and keeping great people, you will get better and better at it. You will become more skillful in your ability to interview and hire. You will become more competent in your ability to manage and motivate. You will become more valuable to yourself and your organization.

As you become better and better at finding great people and turning them into top teams, you will realize your full potential as a manager. There will be no limit to how far you can go or how high you can rise. You will become one of the outstanding executives of the twenty-first century. Good luck!

Learning Resources of Brian Tracy International

MAKE YOUR FIRST MILLION SEMINAR
How to Make Your First Million— or More—in Seven Years or Less

Are you serious about achieving financial independence? Join Brian Tracy for two exciting days to learn how you can make your first million—and more— faster than you ever thought possible.

In this extremely popular, hands-on seminar, you learn a step-by-step process to unlock your hidden potential, make more money, and get out of debt.

You learn how to increase your income, cut your costs, boost your savings, and invest your way to financial independence. You learn the practical, proven methods and strategies used by all self-made millionaires.

You learn how to start and build your own business and develop multiple streams of income that make you financially independent for the rest of your life.

Brian Tracy has taught these principles to more than two million people in twenty-three countries over the past twenty years. In this exciting two-day experience, you will learn a proven system for financial success that can change your life forever.

The entire program is also available in a convenient home study version. For complete details or to register, visit us at www.briantracy.com and click on "Make Your First Million."

BRIAN TRACY AUDIO LEARNING
PROGRAMS

	AUDIO	CD
❖ **Psychology of Achievement** (7 hours) The most popular program on success and achievement in the world.	$65.00	$70.00
❖ **Psychology of Success** (7 hours) The 10 principles of peak performance practiced by all high achievers.	$65.00	$70.00
❖ **Psychology of Selling** (7 hours) The most powerful, practical, professional selling program in the world today.	$75.00	$80.00
❖ **How to Master Your Time** (7 hours) More than 500 key ideas for time management in a proven system that brings about immediate results. Save 2 hours every day.	$65.00	$70.00
❖ **Million-Dollar Habits** (7 hours) The specific habits and behaviors practiced by high earners and self-made millionaires. Double and triple your income.	$65.00	$70.00
❖ **How Leaders Lead** (7 hours) With Ken Blanchard. How to manage, motivate, inspire, and lead a winning team.	$65.00	
❖ **Advanced Selling Techniques** (7 hours) The most complete advanced selling program for top professionals in the world.	$75.00	$80.00
❖ **Master Strategies for High Achievement** (7 hours) More than 150 of the key strategies practiced by the most successful people—in every area of life.	$65.00	$70.00

	AUDIO	CD
❖ **Accelerated Learning Techniques** (7 hours) How to learn faster, remember more, and unlock the power of your mind for maximum performance.	$65.00	$70.00
❖ **Thinking Big** (7 hours) How to dream big dreams, build self-confidence, set goals, and develop the mind-set of successful people.	$65.00	$70.00
❖ **The Luck Factor** (7 hours) More than 60 proven strategies to increase the likelihood that you will be the right person at the right place at the right time.	$65.00	$70.00
❖ **Breaking the Success Barrier** (7 hours) The 12 most powerful thinking tools ever discovered enable you to overcome any obstacle, achieve any goal.	$65.00	$70.00

❖ SPECIAL OFFER ❖

Any 1 program—$65 • 2–3 programs—$60 each

4–5 programs—$55 each • Any 6 programs—$295

Any 10 programs—$450

To order one or more of these programs, phone 800/542-4252, visit our Web site at www.briantracy.com, or write to Brian Tracy International, 462 Stevens Avenue, Suite 202, Solana Beach, CA 92075. Fax: 858/481-2445.

Unconditionally guaranteed for one full year or your money back!

If you are not delighted with these learning programs, return the materials for a complete refund anytime in the year following the date of purchase.

Index

About the Author

BRIAN TRACY is one of the top professional speakers and trainers in the world today. He addresses more than 250,000 men and women each year on the subjects of leadership, strategy, sales, and personal and business success.

Brian is an avid student of business, psychology, management, sales, history, economics, politics, metaphysics, and religion. He brings a unique blend of humor, insight, information, and inspiration to the more than 100 talks and seminars he conducts worldwide each year.

Brian believes that each person has extraordinary untapped potential that he or she can learn to access and, in so doing, accomplish more in a few years than the average person does in a lifetime.

Brian Tracy is the chairman of Brian Tracy International, a human resource development company headquartered in Solana Beach, California. He has written sixteen books and produced more than 300 audio and video training programs. His materials have been translated into twenty languages and are used in thirty-eight countries.

Brian lives with his wife, Barbara, and their four children in Solana Beach, California. He is active in community affairs and serves as a consultant to several nonprofit organizations.

Berrett-Koehler Publishers

Berrett-Koehler is an independent publisher of books, periodicals, and other publications at the leading edge of new thinking and innovative practice on work, business, management, leadership, stewardship, career development, human resources, entrepreneurship, and global sustainability.

Since the company's founding in 1992, we have been committed to supporting the movement toward a more enlightened world of work by publishing books, periodicals, and other publications that help us to integrate our values with our work and work lives, and to create more humane and effective organizations.

We have chosen to focus on the areas of work, business, and organizations, because these are central elements in many people's lives today. Furthermore, the work world is going through tumultuous changes, from the decline of job security to the rise of new structures for organizing people and work. We believe that change is needed at all levels—individual, organizational, community, and global—and our publications address each of these levels.

We seek to create new lenses for understanding organizations, to legitimize topics that people care deeply about but that current business orthodoxy censors or considers secondary to bottom-line concerns, and to uncover new meaning, means, and ends for our work and work lives.

See next pages for other publications from
Berrett-Koehler Publishers